AF436582

CONTENT

Praise for Scott McKain's Previous Books:

"This is further evidence that Scott McKain is the premiere business communicator of our time. Not only has Scott produced extraordinary results in his own businesses by adhering to these principles, but he makes it simple for you to do so as well. By following these easily applied concepts, you will set the standard of excellence for your industry and make your competition irrelevant."

Joseph Michelli, *PhD, speaker, consultant, and author of The Starbucks Experience and The New Gold Standard: 5 Leadership Principles for Creating a Legendary Customer Experience Courtesy of the Ritz-Carlton Hotel Company*

"Differentiation is not an option in business. In a world where the word 'commodity' has become the norm, Scott McKain clarifies the all-important (and all-profitable) strategy to become different, become *distinct*, and become *dominant* in your marketplace. Buy this book. Read it. And put it into practice."

Jeffrey Gitomer, *author of The Little Red Book of Selling*

"Scott McKain's latest book, is a must-read for any professional or organization attempting to creatively differentiate from the competition."

Don Hutson, *co-author of the #1 New York Times bestseller The One Minute Entrepreneur, and CEO of U. S. Learning*

"Scott McKain may just save our sanity and common sense with his positive approach to business and life itself."

"For thirty-one years as an NFL referee, every time I walked off the field, I asked myself if I had left the game better today than I had found it. My intention was to discover ways I could distinguish my performance— not only from others but also from my previous efforts. Scott McKain tells what it takes to be the best you can be, whether you are running a business or refereeing a Super Bowl. I have never read a book that explains it so well. This is a must-read!"

Dr. Jim Tunney, *"Dean of NFL Officials," referee of three Super Bowls, member of NFL Hall of Fame, educator, and author of It's the Will, Not the Skill*

Opening Thought

Several years ago, I heard author, investor, and speaker Joe Calloway (one of my closest friends) tell a highly impactful and inspiring story. You may have already discovered it. Ben Hunt-Davis, a member of the rowing team that won Gold in the 2020 Sydney Olympic Games, has written a book on this unique legend.

This British rowing team set a remarkable goal of winning the Gold Medal in just two years. They achieved this incredible feat by funneling every action and each decision through a single question: "**Does it make the boat go faster?**"

Some ideas or projects might be fine for another time, but because they only had two years to achieve their objective, they purposefully limited their actions to those that made the boat go faster.

Given the current business landscape, we are at a crucial point where our businesses must not just survive but thrive. With more demanding customers than ever, technology advancements like AI leveling the playing field, and more options available in both the B2B and B2C arenas than ever before, time is of the essence.

To succeed, we need to focus all our efforts around this single, urgent question: **How do we get more customers to spend more money more often and give us more referrals?** This is the key. It's the primary problem that your business faces.

Perhaps if we had unlimited time and resources, we could expand our number of questions and have multiple targets. Yet, if you achieve the desired outcome of more frequent customers spending larger sums and providing more referrals, you could also expand the ways you can provide value to your internal and external customers, your stakeholders, and your community.

The way you answer this essential question and solve your primary problem is found on the following pages.

Introduction: The Primary Problem Your Business Faces

Every business, whether a global corporation or a small-town shop, grapples with this one primary problem: **How do we get more customers to spend more money more often and give us more referrals?**

The lifeblood of any and every business is creating customers who grow their loyalty with you and become your advocates in the marketplace.

The solution lies in being chosen more frequently by your target audience. But how do you achieve this?

In today's world, where products and services increasingly look alike, the secret to being chosen more often is creating distinction.

It's not enough to be great; you must stand out. This is true for any industry, from financial services to retail, technology firms to local diners. When everything looks the same to customers, they make their choices based on price alone, and that's a race to the bottom no business can afford to win.

Imagine walking down the Main Street of any city or town. The stores look alike, the products are similar, and even the service feels interchangeable. This homogenization leads to a marketplace where businesses struggle to be noticed. They end up trapped in a vicious cycle of price competition, which erodes their profit margins and stifles innovation. The challenge is clear: to break free from this cycle, businesses must find ways to create meaningful distinctions that resonate with their customers.

It would be difficult to find any professional leader, from CEO to sales consultant, who would vote against standing out and looking better than the competition. Everyone is in favor of it, yet few know how to go about making distinction into reality.

The fact is few organizations really change; instead, they merely shuffle.

They reorganize, add managers, subtract staff, outsource, relocate offices, put more people in the field, and enhance support from the corporate headquarters—all in the hope of engineering advantages they trust will distance themselves from their competition. Such activities, however, rarely create the elements necessary to inspire distinction.

The Promise of This Book

This book will show you how creating distinction in your business will attract more and better customers, setting you apart in a crowded marketplace. You'll learn why standing out is not just an option but a necessity in today's competitive environment. Through practical steps and real-world examples, you'll discover how to identify and enhance the unique qualities that make your business irresistible to customers.

Over the past two decades, I have consulted with and given presentations to some of the world's most innovative companies to create this concept and develop the specific strategies you're about to read. Along with a lengthy and varied career as an author, lecturer, researcher, and consultant, I founded my own profitable businesses.

But I'm not in this to promote my companies; I want to be a catalyst for you to stop and think about yours.

The Challenge and Your Journey

If you want to solve your primary business problem but aren't primed to put in the work, you might as well start getting ready. Your customers will go elsewhere unless you make the required effort to stand out and become more compelling.

If you cannot find it within yourself to become emotional, committed, engaged, and, yes, fervent about solving this primary problem, then you had better be prepared to take your place among that vast multitude of the mediocre who are judged by their customers solely based on price. It is the singularly worst place to be in all of business.

If you aren't willing to create distinction for yourself in your profession and your organization in the marketplace, then take your seat in the back, with the substantial swarm of the similar, where indifference reigns supreme.

Is This Over the Top? No.

If this seems overly dramatic or hyperbolic, just remember your walk down Main Street and the deserted storefronts that once housed businesses of all types. They now sit silently as monuments to the deaths of organizations that have become casualties of the collapse of distinction.

Pick one: Distinction or Extinction

Your journey to distinction starts with understanding the landscape of sameness that permeates the market. It involves recognizing the forces that erode differentiation and learning how to overcome them. By the end of this book, you'll have a clear roadmap for transforming your business into one that stands out and gets chosen more often.

Let's embark on this journey together. You and your business deserve to be noticed and valued for what makes it unique. It's time to step ashore from the sea of sameness and into a world where your business shines as brightly as the coastal sun on a cloudless day.

Welcome to the journey of creating distinction and vanquishing the primary problem your business is facing.

Scott McKain

THE PRIMARY PROBLEM

The Reason Your Business Underperforms Despite Your Best Efforts

Chapter 1:

Understanding the Market Landscape

It's always been there in front of you, but now you've had the "blinding flash of the obvious."

It is what I and many others call the "sea of sameness." And it's not just happening on that Main Street you were walking—it's everywhere: online, B2B as well as B2C, and even in the services we use every day. It's like the whole world has decided that blending in is the way to go.

But here's the problem: when everyone looks the same, how is a customer or prospect supposed to choose? How do you know which business is the right fit?

More often than not, we end up basing our decision on the only thing that seems to differ: the price.

And that -- right there -- is a critical issue. When businesses compete solely on price, it's a race to the bottom. They slash prices, cut corners, and do whatever it takes to stay in the game – even cutting staff members and the service they provide. But in the end, nobody wins— not the businesses and especially not the customers.

When your business fails to create distinction – meaningful, valuable differences that set you apart – you are not just blending in. You're losing out on the chance to connect with your customers on a deeper level. You're missing the opportunity to create loyal fans who will stick with you and refer you to their colleagues and friends.

A study by Bain & Company found that companies that excel in customer experience grow revenues 4-8% above the market average. And a survey by Accenture found that 61% of consumers are more likely to buy from companies that deliver unique content.

What does this tell us? It tells us that distinction matters.

It tells us that businesses that dare to be different and create meaningful and valuable customer experiences will thrive in today's market.

It's Them, Not Me – Right?

I know you might be thinking, "But my business is different! We're not like those other guys."

You're probably right.

But here's the thing: if you're not actively working to create distinction or constantly looking for ways to stand out and deliver value, you risk being swept away by the tides of sameness.

Real-World Examples of Disruption

Automotive Industry:

The "Big Three" carmakers – GM, Ford, and Chrysler – dominated the auto market for many years. They offered similar vehicles with minor variations, and customers bought them up like hotcakes. However, in the 1970s, foreign competitors like Toyota and Honda came along with their unique designs and focus on quality and innovation. Suddenly, the Big Three found themselves struggling to keep up.

Razor Market:

For decades, the razor market was dominated by big players like Gillette and Schick. They offered similar products—multi-blade razors with minor variations in design and features. And for a while, it worked. Customers bought into the idea that more blades equal a better shave, so the brands consistently made incremental product improvements and raked in the profits.

Then came a little company called Dollar Shave Club. Founded in 2011, Dollar Shave Club had a simple premise: deliver high-quality razors to customers' doors for just a few bucks a month. No more overpriced blades, no more trips to the store.

At first, the big brands dismissed DSC. They didn't see Dollar Shave Club as a real threat. But then something interesting happened. Customers started to realize they might not need all those fancy features. Maybe a simple, well-designed razor was enough.

That's when things started to change. Dollar Shave Club's membership grew exponentially, from just a few thousand members in 2012 to over 3 million by 2016. Other startups like Harry's and Billie soon followed suit, offering their spin on the subscription razor model.

The big brands tried to keep up. Gillette launched its subscription service, and Schick lowered its prices. But it was too little, too late. In 2016, Unilever bought Dollar Shave Club for a whopping $1 billion, cementing its place as a significant player in the industry.

The Danger of...

Both examples display the power of distinction. Dollar Shave Club didn't just offer a cheaper product - it offered a completely different experience. It changed the way people thought about buying razors, and it did it in a way that resonated with customers. Foreign automakers altered the way people bought their automobiles.

But these examples also show the danger of complacency. The big brands in cars, razors, and countless other industries got too comfortable with their dominance and failed to innovate. They didn't take the threat of disruption seriously -- until it was too late.

It's a perfect example of why distinction matters. In a world where customers have endless options, businesses must give them a reason to choose them over the competition. They need to offer something unique, something valuable, something that sets them apart.

It's an old cautionary tale, but it's also a lesson. In today's market, distinction isn't a luxury – it's a necessity.

And it starts with understanding your customers and what they truly value.

Statistical Support

According to a McKinsey study, businesses prioritizing customer experience see a 20% increase in customer satisfaction and a 15% increase in sales conversion rates. This statistic underscores the critical role that distinction plays in driving business success.

Creating Distinction

So how do you do it? How do you create distinction in a sea of sameness? We're about to dive in.

- **First and foremost, you need to know your audience.** Who are they? What do they care about? What keeps them up at night? The more you understand your customers, the better equipped you'll be to create experiences that resonate with them.

- **Next, you need to be willing to take risks**. To step outside of your comfort zone and try something new. Because let's face it – if you're doing the same thing as everyone else, you're not really creating distinction, are you?

But it's not just about being different for the sake of being different. Your distinction needs to have meaning and value for your customers. It must solve a problem, fulfill a desire, or make their lives a little easier.

A study by Kantar Millward Brown found that brands with meaningful differences have 7% higher sales growth and 6% higher market share than brands without.

- **And finally, you need to be consistent.** Creating distinction isn't a one-and-done deal – it's an ongoing process that requires commitment and dedication. You need to infuse your unique value into every touchpoint, from your branding and marketing to your customer service and beyond.

This all might sound a bit overwhelming. But the good news is you don't have to go it alone. In the following chapters, we'll dive deeper into the strategies and tactics you can use to create meaningful distinction in your business. We'll explore everything from crafting a compelling brand identity to delivering exceptional customer experiences.

Practical Tips

3 Quick Tips for Standing Out in the Market:

1. ***Know Your Unique Value:*** Identify what sets your business apart from the competition.

2. ***Engage Your Customers:*** Create memorable experiences that resonate with your target audience.

3. ***Innovate Continuously:*** Stay ahead by constantly looking for ways to improve and differentiate your offerings.

But before we get there, I want you to take a moment and think about your own business.

- What makes you unique?

- What inimitable value do you offer your customers?

- And most importantly, how can you communicate that value in a way that resonates?

At the end of the day, this is what it's all about. It's about standing out from that sea of sameness. It's about creating experiences that matter to your customers. And it's about building a business that doesn't just survive but thrives.

Three Crucial Questions

1. Are you ready to be the lighthouse in the storm, the beacon that guides your customers to a better experience?

2. Are you ready to solve the single biggest problem your business faces?

3. Are you ready to create distinction?

Chapter 2:

The Three Destroyers of Differentiation

In today's highly competitive marketplace, businesses often struggle to stand out despite their best efforts. They are inadvertently pulled back into that "sea of sameness," even as they may believe they are doing what it takes to improve profitability and enhance success.

You cannot get customers to spend more money more often and give you more referrals without providing them a reason to do so. If your business is basically the same as your competition, why would they take the actions you desire?

To truly understand how to create distinction, it's essential to understand why it is so rare in today's marketplace.

Several factors can contribute to this phenomenon. Here are three examples:

1. **Fear of taking risks:** Many businesses hesitate to take bold, innovative steps that deviate from industry norms. The fear of failure and the potential financial repercussions often lead companies to play it safe, opting for tried-and-true strategies that have worked for their competitors.

2. **Overemphasis on benchmarking:** While benchmarking can provide valuable insights, an overreliance on this practice can lead businesses to mimic their competitors' strategies, products, and services. Companies risk losing sight of their unique strengths and market positioning by focusing too heavily on what others are doing.

3. **Short-term thinking:** The pressure to deliver quick results and meet short-term targets can hinder businesses from investing in long-term strategies that could set them apart from the competition. This myopic approach often leads to a focus on tactics that provide immediate gains but fail to create sustainable differentiation.

However, my research and experience have brought me to the conclusion that three primary factors create this gravitational pull on your business—and you—to the similarity and commoditization that infect most in the marketplace. That's why this chapter focuses on the Three Destroyers that shaped the collapse of distinction.

Taken individually, each of these Three Destroyers of Differentiation creates a compelling challenge. Combined, they have a synergistic and destructive impact on your industry, your organization, and even upon you professionally and personally. As we navigate the competitive landscape, it becomes clear that the three primary forces that undermine our efforts to stand out are:

1. *Copycat Competition*

2. *Incremental Advancement Because of Tougher Competition*

3. *Complacency*

These destroyers of differentiation have a profound impact on businesses, eroding their uniqueness and leaving them vulnerable in a crowded market.

Destroyer 1: Copycat Competition

In our competitive society, the natural inclination is to imitate the success of others. When a competitor introduces a new feature or strategy, businesses rush to replicate it, hoping to capture the same success. However, this approach leads to a market where everyone looks the same. True differentiation requires innovation, not imitation. It demands a focus on what sets your business apart rather than what the competition does.

If you surpass me with a novel approach or tactic, my instinctive reaction is to duplicate it. If I can replicate your work, my customers will easily conclude that you no longer possess a competitive edge.

Suppose your innovative approach has resulted in substantial success in the market. In that case, it seems logical to try to replicate the factors that contributed to your advantage and perhaps attempt to marginally do you one better.

Over time, this strategy is anything but safe!

Instead, we mutually undermine any points of uniqueness that could improve our separate companies and better serve our customers. Our attention appears to be focused on competitors in the same industry that provide comparable services and make comparable products rather than customers, all the while engaging in the internal political games that are a part of every company.

Example: The Smartphone Industry

Take the smartphone industry, for instance. For years, manufacturers have quickly copied each other's designs and features. Apple introduced the iPhone with its sleek design and touch screen, and soon after, every major smartphone manufacturer released their version of a touch-screen phone. While some managed to incorporate unique features, many simply mimicked the iPhone's look and feel.

However, companies like Samsung eventually realized that to truly stand out, they needed to innovate beyond just copying. With its larger screen and stylus, Samsung's introduction of the Galaxy Note series created a new category of smartphones that appealed to a different market segment. This bold move paid off, helping Samsung establish itself as a leader in the smartphone market, not just another iPhone imitator.

Research and Statistics

According to a report by Deloitte, companies that focus on innovation are more likely to experience higher growth rates. The study found that the most innovative companies achieved a growth rate of 20% or more, compared to only 5% for the least innovative companies. This data underscores the importance of innovation over imitation in achieving sustainable growth. (We will discuss innovation and creativity in more depth in a later chapter.)

Destroyer 2: Incremental Advancement Because of Tougher Competition

Many businesses fall into the trap of making small, incremental improvements, believing these minor tweaks will set them apart.

While incremental advancements can provide temporary gains, they rarely lead to significant differentiation.

I think of my hometown diner and its response after the opening of the first nearby McDonald's many years ago. Seemingly in the blink of an eye, Alvie Kern of Crothersville, Indiana—and thousands of small business owners just like him across the United States—was in severe economic trouble for the first time in his entrepreneurial life. He was confronted with competition he had never imagined in his wildest dreams. He was facing rivals that barely existed, as far as he knew, just a few years earlier. In those days, your competition was another restaurant a few blocks away, not a national chain in every community.

Put yourself in Alvie's shoes for a moment. You are not a businessperson, no matter what your hometown believes. You are a sandwich person.

This is a perfect example of a phenomenon of many organizations— and particularly small businesses. A guy starts a sporting goods store not because he sees an opening in the marketplace or a chance to be distinctive. Instead, he's a local jock who wants to stay involved in sports. I've done lots of work lately in the automotive body shop industry, meeting many owners of car repair shops who got into the business because they wanted to fix cars—not because of any particular business acumen.

I still remember Alvie constantly grousing in his cigarette-induced gravelly voice that he didn't understand how "anyone could eat that McDonald's junk"—all the while losing business to the chain in droves. His approach was to try to "out-McDonald McDonald's" by attempting to incrementally improve on what THEY were doing instead of emphasizing the small-town diner aspects that made his place distinctive.

Sure, he knew hamburgers – but product knowledge and industry commitment were insufficient. Something additional—something distinctive—is required if you are to cinch a triumph.

To stand out, businesses must embrace bold, innovative changes that capture their customers' imaginations.

It's about thinking uniquely and taking risks others are unwilling to accept.

What could Alvie have done? Instead of trying to get you out the door just as quickly as McDonald's could, he might have tried an approach that emphasized coming in, having a sandwich or cup of coffee, and getting some work done outside your home or office. (It sure worked years later for Starbucks!) In other words, rather than trying to be incrementally better than the new competition, he should have emphasized what Kern's Grill had as potential advantages that McDonald's didn't. More variety in the menu, a place to sit, talk, and relax, each meal prepared especially for your order, support for the local community, and additional advantages were ignored – all in the effort to make your trip to his restaurant as speedy as McDonald's. Let's be clear – it might not have worked...but distinction was Alvie Kern's only shot at surviving and thriving in the new competitive marketplace.

Sadly, Kern's Grill closed its doors shortly thereafter.

Example: The Automotive Industry

The automotive industry, once again, provides a clear example – this time of the dangers of incremental advancement. For decades, traditional car manufacturers made minor yearly improvements to their vehicles – slightly better fuel efficiency, marginally improved safety features, or minor design tweaks. While these incremental advancements kept the product line fresh, they didn't fundamentally change the market.

In contrast, Tesla took a bold approach by revolutionizing the electric vehicle market. Instead of making minor improvements, Tesla redefined what a car could be. The introduction of the Model S, with its impressive range, advanced autopilot features, and over-the-air software updates, was but one of many moves that set Tesla apart from traditional manufacturers. This bold, innovative approach helped Tesla become a leader in the electric vehicle market. And while this marketplace – like every other one in history – is constantly evolving, growing, and changing, the head start that Tesla has created over competitors gives it an advantage.

We can debate Elon Musk's mercurial behavior based on our respective personal opinions. However, as of this writing, Tesla's market capitalization is ten times that of General Motors. The question of whether it will maintain its leadership position is really all about whether it will continue to create distinction or succumb to these destroyers.

Research and Statistics

A Boston Consulting Group study found that companies prioritizing breakthrough innovation over incremental improvements are more likely to achieve market leadership. The research indicated that firms focusing on radical innovation are 2.5 times more likely to be among the top performers in their industry compared to those that focus on incremental changes.

Destroyer 3: Complacency

My mother constantly said, "Familiarity breeds contempt."

As much as I hate to contradict my mother's advice, my experience has taught me that this one is incorrect. Becoming well acquainted with someone does not imply that you become scornful of them.

We become complacent, assuming it will always be there.

We witness this frequently in our daily lives. Unfortunately, we often take for granted those closest to us. For example, we do not plan to disrespect our spouses or partners. However, a continuous drift toward complacency appears to be a component of the human condition.

Perhaps we assume that if something or someone is overwhelmingly familiar, it represents a garden that no longer requires our enthusiastic or methodical attention. We might mistakenly believe, for example, that our spouse or partner's love will always be there and that it does not require the same level of cultivation, intensity, or time commitment as something we have yet to acquire.

Over time, even successful businesses can become complacent, taking their customers for granted and assuming their current strategies will continue to work. This complacency breeds stagnation and erodes customer loyalty. In today's fast-paced market, businesses must continually innovate and improve to keep their customers engaged and satisfied. It requires a proactive approach and a commitment to excellence.

Example: The Retail Industry

Consider the case of Sears. Once a retail giant, Sears became complacent, failing to adapt to the changing retail landscape. While competitors like Walmart and Amazon embraced e-commerce and digital innovation, Sears continued to rely on its traditional brick-and-mortar model. This complacency led to a steady decline in market share, ultimately resulting in bankruptcy.

On the other hand, Walmart recognized the threat posed by Amazon and took proactive steps to adapt. Walmart invested heavily in its online presence, acquiring e-commerce companies like Jet.com and integrating digital technologies into its operations. These efforts have helped Walmart remain competitive and continue to grow in a rapidly changing retail environment.

Research and Statistics

According to a report by McKinsey & Company, companies that fail to adapt to changing market conditions are more likely to experience declining performance. The study found that 75% of companies that do not prioritize continuous innovation see a decrease in profitability over time. This highlights the critical need for businesses to remain proactive and avoid complacency.

The Down-Low on Destroyers

In my book, What Customers REALLY Want, I write that every organization or professional on the planet has some kind of acquisition strategy; in other words, almost all of us have some sort of specific plan for attracting new customers.

However, few companies or professionals have a retention strategy, a program planned with equal precision and passion that outlines specific steps for retaining current customers and growing and expanding the business we are obtaining from them.

The ideal analogy for customer retention and growth is our personal lives.

A great way to strengthen a relationship, according to any marriage counselor, is to keep romancing the person who has already promised to be your life partner.

When dating, we do everything it takes to keep the spark alive. We communicate via text and phone and send notes, gifts, and emails. We go above and beyond the typical dating routine, attempting to surprise and delight our future significant other with little, unexpected gestures.

For many couples, the "I do" is the final step of the courtship. Unfortunately, for many – perhaps most – couples, the romance in the relationship then wanes over time.

The same is true in business. For some strange reason, it seems we value—and are more enthusiastic about "courting"—our prospects more than we value our current customers. We are always looking for new ones, often at the expense of the existing ones.

Understanding these destroyers is crucial for recognizing why meaningful differentiation is rare and what challenges must be overcome to achieve distinction for both your current customers – to maintain and grow their business with you – and the prospects you seek to attract. By addressing these forces head-on, you can begin to create a business that stands out and gets chosen more often.

What are you doing – right now – to inspire your existing customers? **Remember: your best customers are your competitor's best prospects.** If you won't romance them, someone else will.

Key Takeaways

1. Innovation Over Imitation: Focus on what sets your business apart rather than copying competitors.

2. Embrace Bold Changes: Aim for revolutionary improvements that capture customer imagination.

3. Avoid Complacency: Continuously innovate and adapt to stay ahead in a fast-paced market.

By understanding and addressing these destroyers of differentiation, you can create a unique and valuable presence in the market, ensuring long-term success and customer loyalty.

In the next chapter, we will begin our exploration of the Four Cornerstones of Distinction and how they can transform your business and provide the solution to your primary problem.

Chapter 3:

The Four Cornerstones of Distinction – Cornerstone #1: Clarity

Through my research and experience, I discovered Four Cornerstones of Distinction. Every business and individual should use these Cornerstones to differentiate themselves and solve their primary problem.

These Cornerstones will at first appear to be fundamental. However, the more you study them   and what is required to be effective at each—the more you will realize how extraordinarily difficult it is to put them into practice.

When you think about it, this paradox may also answer an important question: *Why is true distinction so rare?*

The answer is that we either don't recognize or understand these fundamentals, or we fail to design and implement the strategies and tactics required to carry them out—or both.

The good news is that every company or professional can immediately improve their situation. When you uncover the Cornerstones of Distinction, you can immediately start planning how you will use their power.

The First of the Four Cornerstones: CLARITY

Clarity is the cornerstone of any successful business. It involves precisely understanding who you are, what you do, and what makes you unique. Without clarity, your marketing messages can become muddled, and your value proposition can be lost on potential customers. In this chapter, we will explore the importance of clarity, how to achieve it, and how it can transform your business. We will delve into defining your Clarity Statement, ensuring employee alignment, and consistently communicating your uniqueness in the marketplace. Throughout, we will draw on current examples, research, and statistics to support these points.

The Importance of Clarity

In a marketplace saturated with similar products and services, clarity is what sets successful businesses apart. Clarity helps you define your brand, align your team, and communicate effectively with your customers. When you clearly understand your identity and value proposition, you can create focused strategies that resonate with your target audience.

Many organizations and professionals are terrified of losing to the competition, so they strive to become almost all things to almost all people, believing it will bring them more customers.

Play a game sometime with someone in financial services, for example. All you need to do is innocently ask, "What do you do?"

Chances are, she will respond with a litany of products— "I ensure your future with a variety of mutual funds, annuities, IRAs, and other investment instruments, as well as provide total financial solutions including everything from mortgages to retirement planning"—or she will respond with the hot catchphrase for the current market: "I'm a wealth manager." (Some may say "wealth advisor.")

Here's the problem. In the first instance, she isn't telling you who she is; she is informing you about *what she sells*.

And in the second instance, she is really saying precisely the same thing—just in a more polished manner.

With someone in the second group, you can follow up by asking, "How much wealth does one have to invest to become the recipient of your management and advice?"

She will probably view this as an opening and respond, "With a minimum of $100,000 or $250,000 or $500,000 or $1 million (or whatever number she feels comfortable throwing out), I assist my clients by providing -- ready for this? -- a variety of mutual funds, annuities, IRAs, and other investment instruments, as well as providing total financial solutions including everything from mortgages to retirement planning."

These responses are basically all the <u>same</u>. It's just that the second version is slightly more sophisticated—or maybe it's merely slick.

Although this example focuses on one industry, I don't believe the situation is remarkably different in any other field.

- Abundant auto dealers want to accentuate the car's accouterments, believing that constitutes their business rather than enhancing a driver's delight.

- Countless chefs center on their culinary creations instead of the real purpose of their business—developing and intensifying customer connections.

- Plenty of pharmacists pontificate on pills—because their training has centered on the medicine—rather than becoming passionate about patients.

Let me be abundantly emphatic: "Who you are" is <u>*not*</u> what you sell!

"Who you are" must be the distinctive value you bring to the customer, which compels them to do business with you more often, spend more money, and refer you more frequently to their colleagues and friends.

The problem is, you cannot be a "me *too!*" and create distinction in your field.

The top financial advisors I have worked with are highly specialized. For example, they work *exclusively* with surgeons. My friend, Dr. Rick Jensen—a leading sports psychologist who also coaches and consults with financial advisors—knows one professional who works only with PGA golfers and another who works only with people involved in the sport of polo.

If you have a pool of cash to invest but are not a part of the polo scene, this advisor will refer you to someone else. (And, according to Dr. Jensen, he *has!*) Jensen also reports that by turning away the business that is not a good fit, these distinctive financial advisors have become among the most profitable professionals in their industry.

Suppose I focus on surgeons, for example, as my clearly defined client base. In that case, I can learn their schedules, participate in their charitable activities, understand their unique professional challenges, educate myself in some of their specialized terminology, host client events that appeal to their specific needs, plan my work hours to fit the times that are easiest to contact them and be contacted by them, and much more.

However, this also answers why so few in any (and every) profession attain significant distinction.

Can you imagine how difficult it is to learn all this and more about a specific customer base? Therefore, we usually end up—organizationally and individually—knowing our *products* but not our customers. We're often a mile wide and an inch deep when it comes to knowing what would really make a difference for the very people we seek to serve. Or we try to serve so many that we genuinely engage very few.

The truth is you don't have enough time or energy to create highly distinctive customer experiences for a widely varied assembly of wildly diverse customers.

On the other hand, you might say that Walmart sells "everything to everybody"—but that would not be accurate.

What if you want a tuxedo or a designer gown? You cannot find them at Walmart. Walmart is clearly all about marketing low prices every day on mass-market consumer items. There is a sizable amount of clarity regarding who the company is, even though it handles thousands of items.

*Part of the reason clarity is so vital is this: **You cannot differentiate a generic.***

Professionals cannot provide the clarity and intense differentiation required for ultimate success if their focus is diluted. In medicine, for example, we take for granted that the specialist is more highly compensated than the general practitioner. Usually, specialists are not the ones giving referrals to the GPs; it's the other way around. Why would we presume other industries would have a different set of rules?

How About Your Team?

As we discuss the importance of clarity, let's agree from the outset that it's not only the CEO, owner, or managers who must understand this cornerstone. It must be integrated throughout your organization so that it becomes a part of the DNA of your business.

Clarity is not just about what you communicate externally but also about ensuring that everyone within your organization understands and embraces your mission, vision, and unique value proposition. When employees are aligned with your company's goals and values, they become more motivated and effective in their roles.

Employee engagement is closely tied to clarity. When employees understand the company's mission and vision, they are more likely to feel connected to their work and motivated to contribute to its success.

According to a Deloitte study, organizations with a strong sense of purpose experience 30% higher levels of innovation and 40% higher levels of workforce retention.

Effective internal communication is critical to achieving employee alignment. Communicate your clarity regularly through meetings, training sessions, and company-wide communications. Encourage open dialogue and ensure employees have a platform to share their ideas and feedback.

Therefore, as we discuss these concepts, consider how you will integrate them throughout your organization, including the frontline team members or customer service representatives who interact with your customers every day. In today's rapidly changing world, you also need to consider how you will ensure that your AI technology is trained and aligned with your newfound organizational and individual clarity.

Research and Statistics

A Gallup study found that only 41% of employees know what their company stands for and what makes it different from competitors. This lack of clarity can lead to inconsistent messaging and missed opportunities to connect with customers.

In contrast, companies with clear and well-communicated values and goals see a 27% increase in performance and a 50% increase in employee engagement.

Defining Your Clarity Statement

Your Clarity Statement is the foundation of your business's distinction. It defines your purpose, goals, and the unique value you offer. A well-crafted Clarity Statement explains why your company exists and what you hope to achieve in the future.

Consider three fundamental questions as you develop your Clarity Statement:

1. *What makes your business (or you) different from your competition?*

2. *What makes you better than your competition?*

3. *What makes you and your organization unique?*

The Clarity Statement

Your Clarity Statement should be concise, clear, and inspirational. It should reflect your core values and guide your decision-making processes. A strong statement aligns your team and helps customers understand your purpose.

Example: Bombas

Bombas, a sock and apparel company, has a statement that reads, "To help those in need." For every item purchased, Bombas donates an item to those in need. This clear and purposeful mission has driven Bombas' business decisions and marketing strategies, creating a solid brand identity focused on giving back.

Example: TOMS

TOMS' vision is "to use business to improve lives." This clarity has driven the company to innovate and expand its giving model beyond shoes to include eyewear, clean water, and safe birth services. TOMS' clarity in its vision has helped it maintain a strong social impact focus and grow its business.

Additional Clarity Statement Considerations

Your Clarity Statement could also explain how your product or service solves customers' problems or improves their situation, delivers specific benefits, and tells the ideal customer why they should buy from you and not from the competition. Consistently communicating this clarity across all channels is crucial for building a strong brand identity and attracting the right customers.

To improve your Clarity Statement, consider the following steps:

1. **Identify Your Target Audience:** Understand who your ideal customers are and what they value.

2. **Understand Their Pain Points:** Identify your customers' specific problems or challenges.

3. **Highlight Your Unique Solution:** Clearly explain how your product or service addresses these pain points better than the competition.

4. **Emphasize Benefits:** Focus on the tangible benefits and outcomes

customers will experience by choosing your product or service.

Consistent Communication

We will discuss more about communication in a later chapter, but it should be noted here that consistency is vital when it comes to clarity. Clarity plays a crucial role in your marketing efforts. Clear, concise messaging helps potential customers quickly understand what your business offers and why it is valuable. This is particularly important in today's fast-paced digital environment, where consumers have limited attention spans.

Ensure your messaging is uniform across all marketing channels, including your website, social media, advertising, and customer communications. Consistent messaging reinforces your brand identity and helps build trust with your audience.

Example: Dropbox

Dropbox's messaging is clear and straightforward: "Keep life organized and work moving—all in one place." This simple statement communicates the core benefit of using Dropbox, making it easy for potential customers to understand its value. Dropbox's clarity in messaging has helped it become a leader in the cloud storage market.

Example: Allbirds

Allbirds consistently communicates its commitment to sustainability and comfort across all channels. From its website to its social media presence and advertising campaigns, Allbirds' messaging reinforces its brand values and mission. This clarity has helped Allbirds build a strong global brand and a loyal customer base.

Measuring the Impact of Cornerstone #1

Measuring the impact of your clarity efforts is essential to ensure their effectiveness. Use qualitative and quantitative metrics to assess how well employees and customers understand and embrace your Clarity Statement. Here are three steps to take:

1. **Employee Surveys:** Conduct regular surveys to gauge employee understanding and alignment with the company's clarity. Use this feedback to identify areas for improvement in communication and ensure that all employees are on the same page.

2. **Customer Feedback:** Gather customer feedback to understand how well they perceive and understand your clarity proposition. Use surveys, focus groups, and customer reviews to gain insights into their experience with your brand.

3. **Performance Metrics:** Track key performance indicators (KPIs) such as customer acquisition, retention rates, and brand loyalty. Analyze how your clarity initiatives impact these metrics and adjust your strategies accordingly.

Example: REI

REI, the outdoor retail co-op, regularly measures the impact of its clarity initiatives through employee and customer surveys. The company gathers feedback to ensure alignment with its mission to "inspire, educate, and outfit for a lifetime of outdoor adventure and stewardship." REI's focus on clarity has helped it build a strong brand and achieve high levels of customer satisfaction.

Example: Warby Parker

Warby Parker, the eyewear retailer, is another example of a company that excels in clarity. Warby Parker's mission is "to offer designer eyewear at a revolutionary price while leading the way for socially conscious businesses." This is clearly communicated through its marketing, customer service, and corporate social responsibility initiatives.

Warby Parker's vision (pardon the pun) of providing affordable, high-quality eyewear is supported by its unique business model of direct-to-consumer sales and its commitment to donating a pair of glasses for every pair sold. The company's clarity in its mission and vision has resonated with customers, driving its rapid growth and success.

Clarity is More Than the Total Organization

The idea of a Clarity Statement should not be limited to a broad application focusing on the total organization.

As I've suggested, individuals also need this as a starting point on the road to the clarity necessary to build distinction. In addition, if you seek to create distinction within your company—for your department, for example—a Clarity Statement is a terrific place to begin.

Several years ago, I was the keynote speaker for the annual meeting of the American Payroll Association, which is led by its dynamic and highly creative CEO, Dan Maddux.

The challenge I addressed for the group was that most employees in their departments would probably define their jobs as merely "cutting payroll checks." Let's face it; few people become motivated and excited about going to the office and creating distinction by simply "cutting checks."

Now, however, several of the payroll departments of the organizations in attendance have signs on the walls of their offices with their new, distinctive Clarity Statement: "We deposit the money that funds the dreams of thousands of families—including our own!" They're not merely cutting checks; they're *funding dreams!*

Many will undoubtedly read about determining a simple Clarity Statement and consider the exercise futile in today's volatile economy. They may feel it is corny and childish to provide platitudes that accomplish little in the way of profitability and sales.

I'm afraid I obviously have to disagree. I believe your Clarity Statement is the *starting point of the development of distinction*.

Clarity is the foundation of distinction.

Clarity involves precisely understanding who you are, what you do, and what makes you unique. By defining this and ensuring all employees understand and can articulate what makes your business distinctive, as well as consistently communicating your distinct value proposition, you can create a company that stands out and attracts more and better customers. The journey to distinction begins with clarity, and its impact can be profound and far-reaching.

Example: High Point University

A close friend of many years is Dr. Nido Qubein, President of High Point University. A member of the executive committee and board of directors of financial giant Truist and the chairman of the board of Great Harvest Bread Company, Qubein was already a multimillionaire businessman, author, and speaker when he decided to make a significant difference for his alma mater and accepted the offer to become the university's leader.

One of the first aspects Qubein introduced to the institution was initiating an effort to become extraordinarily precise about its points of differentiation, thereby beginning to create clarity and distinction.

Consider HPU's competition for students for a moment: within just a few miles are nationally renowned institutions of higher learning such as Duke University, the University of North Carolina (UNC), and Wake Forest. Just a little farther down the road is North Carolina State University. How could a small college like HPU compete against UNC and the others?

First, upon assuming the duties of the presidency, Qubein created a Clarity Statement for his university. It's a brilliant one that both students and parents love:

"At High Point University, every student receives an extraordinary education in an inspiring environment with caring people."

Who would not want to be a part of that?

However, the depth of the statement is also easy to overlook. It requires the university to deliver on this promise to every student, not just those receiving scholarships or studying at an honors level.

The education must be extraordinary—not simply the certification of a degree—and that's a pretty tall order when considering the competitive atmosphere for the best students available.

And although many of us may remember challenging academic times during our college years or having fun with new friends, I doubt a significant portion of us would state that our institution of higher learning was also totally committed to creating an "inspiring environment." Yet High Point University makes that pledge to its prospective and current students.

Finally, HPU vows to students and their parents that the faculty and staff consist of "caring people." I imagine your experience in college was similar to mine. Some exceptional professors routinely expressed intense concern for their students, while others didn't care whether they passed or failed. At High Point University, caring people create differentiation.

High Point University will be an example we will visit again and examine its results. Remember, clarity is only the first cornerstone. Dr. Qubein and HPU will have to put several more stones in place to truly differentiate their institution and achieve distinction; however, this is a vitally important process to begin to execute.

Remember, you cannot differentiate what you cannot define.

Therefore, your goal is to be as precise as possible about who you are, what your organization is, and what it is not. Be ready to fire prospects and customers who fail to fit your format.

Clarity is essential because those same customers will not present you with multiple opportunities to define yourself. After dealing with so many non-distinct organizations and professionals, they are vowing, in the lyrics of the old song by The Who, they "won't get fooled again."

The Three Critical Questions for Clarity

1. *What are your values – what do you stand for?*

2. *What are you NOT in your marketplace – what won't you stand for or business you would turn away?*

3. *What makes you unique?*

However, you can be clear about who and what you are—and clearly be boring!

If you cannot engage your colleagues, customers, and prospects, how can you expect them to perceive that you have created distinction?

That's why moving to the second Cornerstone of Distinction is critical: creativity! In the next chapter, we will explore how to foster innovation within your organization, use creative strategies to captivate your audience and set your business apart from the competition to solve your primary problem.

Chapter 4:

The Four Cornerstones of Distinction: Cornerstone #2: CREATIVITY

You can possess extraordinary clarity about your organization and yourself—and still bore your customers to death!

Being precise about what you are—and are not—is a terrific beginning step. However, it is not the sole necessity for building distinction and solving your primary problem.

Creativity Is Second

Visualize a novelist sitting down at her laptop and starting to type. Could you picture her not knowing what the book would be about?

Obviously, the answer is NO. In other words, even as the most innovative artists begin to produce the fruits of their imagination, they are already clear about what they are creating.

Clarity about the work comes before creativity inside the work.

An author does not begin writing without first determining whether she is working on a novel, movie, song lyrics, or poem. No matter how wild her vision is, the artist nonetheless acknowledges, to some extent, the limitations of the genre she has chosen. Songs, as simple as it may appear, require notes; paintings usually use brushes and canvas; novels rely on words.

However, much of the difficulty I've noticed arises when firms push their employees to "think outside the box." They intuitively feel that creativity is enhanced in the absence of restraints. However, as demonstrated above, even the most inventive artists recognize that all forms have inherent constraints. This is why cultivating creativity is the second Cornerstone of distinction.

Creativity without clarity is devoid of distinction

The Role of Creativity in Business

Creativity is not just restricted to artistic expression; it's about problem-solving and developing new methods to meet customer needs. It involves questioning the status quo and daring to be different. Creativity is the key to standing out in a world where products and services increasingly look alike.

Creativity leads to groundbreaking ideas, revolutionary products, and memorable customer experiences when harnessed effectively. This chapter will explore why creativity is critical for distinction, how it fosters innovation, and how businesses can cultivate a creative culture. We will support this discussion with case studies and research, illustrating the transformative power of creativity in business.

Caution: Creativity Ahead!

In discussing the Cornerstone of Creativity, it's crucial to clarify that "creativity" and "innovation" do not necessitate being on the "bleeding edge" of change. This doesn't mean you must commit entirely to the risk of an untested yet potentially disruptive approach or technology. Instead, I advocate the continuous pursuit of new and unique ways to serve customers. Frequently, I observe companies taking excessive risks—often more to impress competitors than to connect with their customers. As we will explore in this chapter, creativity often involves borrowing an idea from a different industry and adapting it to suit your own.

Consider Apple. While it's a frequently cited example in business discussions on innovation, it's instructive to note that Apple didn't invent the personal computer, it didn't create the graphical user interface, others pioneered MP3 music players, and they were relatively late to the game of manufacturing mobile phones. What Apple excels at is taking existing products or features and creatively enhancing them to serve customers in a more distinctive and valuable way. This is a strategy worth considering for your own business.

Creativity vs. Innovation

Often, I'm asked, "Are the terms' innovation' and 'creativity' two ways of expressing the same concept?" As imprecise as my answer is, here is how I look at the issue.

- **Creativity is the spark that ignites innovation.**

    o   It is what leads to transformative changes in the market.

- **Innovation is the application of creative ideas to generate value.**

    o   It involves developing new products, services, processes, or business models that provide a competitive edge.

Example: Spotify

Spotify revolutionized the music industry by leveraging creativity and innovation. Before Spotify, music lovers were restricted to purchasing individual songs or albums. Spotify introduced a new business model with its streaming service, allowing users to access a vast music library for a subscription fee. This creative approach disrupted the traditional music distribution model and transformed how people consume music. With advancements such as personalized playlists and increasingly sophisticated algorithms, Spotify's continuous innovation keeps it ahead of the competition.

"But I'm Not Creative!"

Before we spend too much time on the subject, let's examine how you can become more creative.

Countless authors offer ideas on how a professional or an organization can become more creative. Amazon lists nearly 50,000 books when you search for "creativity and business" and over 70,000 when you search for creativity alone. It would seem from all the discussion that creativity must be a problematic science—but that's not so.

The co-director of Harvard University's Project Zero study of cognitive skills in the sciences and humanities, David N. Perkins, has said creativity "has little to do with intelligence, talent, or expertise. These may provide the raw horsepower for creative endeavors, but not the steering."

In other words, *everyone* can do it.

Here are three approaches for generating and guiding creativity that we will use within the parameters of the clarity we have previously established.

Creative Idea #1: Believe You Are Creative

One of my favorite sayings comes from the book A Whack on the Side the *Head* by Roger von Oech. He states that the key to creativity is simply believing you are. That's it!

When someone protests, "But I'm not creative," the process immediately shuts down. The moment you tell yourself that you cannot be creative, you build a dam across the free flow of ideas. However, people who believe they are creative can easily begin generating ideas and concepts.

Creative Idea #2: Expose Yourself to Stimulus

Another question you must ask yourself is, "Am I being exposed to enough stimulus to generate creativity?"

My friend Randy Gage is a remarkable person who has risen from being a high school dropout to now earning acclaim as the "Millionaire Messiah" because his strategies have assisted so many of his clients in creating wealth. Randy has been quoted as saying:

> *"Creative people generally are self-motivated, independent, delighted by novelty, risk takers, tolerant of ambiguity, deeply involved in their work, avid readers, and world travelers. These characteristics provide creative people with a very rich diet of stimulation, variety, and situations. They see the same thing handled in many different ways, so it opens up the mind to problem-solving, lateral thinking, and innovation."*

Ask yourself right now, "Have I put myself on a very rich diet of stimulation?" If not, what action will you take to do so?

Creative Idea #3: Understand That Creativity Is Synergistic

If one phrase in business jargon has been overused, it is "synergy," which refers to a greater-than-the-sum consequence produced by the interaction of two or more forces. We frequently group people or departments for no apparent reason other than rationalization or the expectation that the move will result in "synergy."

Organizations purchase a competitor and assure Wall Street that the combination will result in higher earnings because of the new synergies. And many times, investors have been extremely disappointed with the results.

Nonetheless, if there is one area where this approach does work, it is innovation. For some strange reason, creativity is difficult in a vacuum. Ideas are enhanced when shared with others.

However, don't assume you must associate with others to develop creative ideas and solutions! While a significant body of research suggests that interaction with others can enhance creativity, there is also evidence that points to the potential benefits of solitude for creative thinking.

- A 2015 study by Chia-Hua Chiu found that social interactions can sometimes impair creativity by leading to cognitive fixation, where people get stuck on a particular idea and have difficulty thinking of new ones. The study suggests that spending time alone may help individuals break free from fixation and generate more novel ideas.

- A 2012 study by Gregory J. Feist found that many highly creative people, particularly in the arts and sciences, tend to be more introverted and solitary. The study suggests that solitude may provide the time and space necessary for deep reflection and the development of original ideas.

- A 2003 study by Mihaly Csikszentmihalyi, a pioneer in the study of creativity, found that creative individuals often alternate between periods of social interaction and solitude. The study suggests that while social interaction can provide inspiration and feedback, solitude is necessary for the hard work of developing and refining creative ideas.

These studies don't necessarily suggest that social interaction always hinders creativity or that solitude is always better. Many studies have found that collaboration and diverse perspectives can lead to more creative solutions. Ultimately, the relationship between social interaction and creativity is complex and may depend on factors such as the nature of the creative task, the personalities of the individuals involved, and the specific dynamics of the social interaction.

A word of caution, however: be careful about who you choose to invite to become a part of your creativity group. We all know those people who brighten a room when they leave it! We are looking for those willing to debate and challenge but not those who respond negatively simply to assert a degree of influence or power. Don't bring creativity killers into your circle of synergy.

A mix of solitude and social interaction may be optimal for many creative endeavors.

Cultivating a Creative Culture

To harness the power of creativity, your business must cultivate a culture that encourages and supports creative thinking. This involves creating an environment where your team feels safe expressing ideas, experimenting, and taking risks.

Encouraging experimentation is crucial for fostering creativity. Employees should feel empowered to test new ideas without fear of failure. Creating a "fail-fast" culture, where quick iterations and learning from failures are valued, can drive innovation.

Even a workplace's physical and cultural environment can significantly impact creativity. Creating spaces that inspire and facilitate collaboration can stimulate creative thinking. Designing workspaces that are open, flexible, and conducive to collaboration can encourage creative interactions. Incorporating elements like natural light, vibrant colors, and comfortable seating can create an environment that stimulates creativity.

Example: LEGO

LEGO is a prime example of leveraging diverse perspectives to drive creativity. The company actively seeks input from its global community of users through platforms like LEGO Ideas, where fans can submit and vote on new product ideas. This collaborative approach has resulted in successful products like the LEGO Women of NASA set. By embracing diverse perspectives, LEGO continues to innovate and captivate its audience.

Example: 3M

3M is renowned for its innovative culture, which has led to the creation of iconic products like Post-it Notes. 3 M's "15% rule" allows employees to spend 15% of their time on projects of their choosing, fostering a culture of experimentation and creativity. This policy has resulted in numerous breakthrough innovations and has cemented 3 M's reputation as a leader in innovation.

Example: Pixar Animation Studios

Pixar Animation Studios is known for its creative work environment. The company's headquarters are designed to encourage spontaneous interactions and collaboration. Open spaces, communal areas, and playful elements like scooters and themed meeting rooms create an atmosphere that fosters creativity. This creative environment has been instrumental in producing numerous critically acclaimed and commercially successful animated films, including the original and sequels of *Toy Story, Cars,* and more.

Investing in Your Team for Creativity

As you might imagine, investing in your work environment only stimulates the creativity and innovation you seek if you also invest in your team – and yourself!

Investing in the creative development of employees can drive innovation and set a company apart. Providing opportunities for learning, growth, and creative expression can unlock the full potential of the workforce. Encouraging continuous learning and professional development can keep employees' skills and knowledge up-to-date. Offering workshops, training programs, and access to creative resources can foster a culture of innovation.

Stimulating Productive Creativity

If you are going to inspire productive creativity—the kind that can stimulate strategies that will have an immediate positive impact on you and your organization—here are the three action steps you should take.

Step One: Drive It Down

Your first step is to use your clarity to break down all customer interactions into the smallest units or steps possible.

Ask yourself this question: what is every point of contact a customer has with me or my organization? Make an extremely detailed list.

During the Q&A session at a recent program in Portland, Oregon, one audience member remarked that her company had "kind of forgotten that our product has to be installed." When I asked her for more insight into her problem, she continued, "We sell business communication systems that include everything from the actual telephone handsets to the service for telephone, wireless, Internet, and television. We have many wonderful advantages that our sales team works hard to communicate. Yet, we never included the installers in this process.

Therefore, we are getting frequent complaints that our technicians aren't creating positive experiences for our customers."

She captured the essence of why it is so important to keep "driving it down" (Step One). Although many organizations are highly aware of the quality of communication between the salesperson and the customer, not nearly as many consider the impact of other representatives on the customer experience.

Now, the critical question: What happens when customers are in contact with you?

It's time to be very specific about the process. If you are like most organizations—or professionals—you aren't finding too much in the way of differentiation.

Step Two: Pick a Point

Now that you know that every one of these specific items is an opening for you to create space between your organization and your competition, the next step is to review each point of contact to ascertain where you can develop differentiation.

Unfortunately, often, the most significant areas of differentiation that most customers observe are merely in logos and color schemes.

In the rental car world, we know that Hertz is yellow, Avis is red, and National is green. But does that have to be the case? Aren't there other meaningful ways to engage clients that would help ensure repeat business?

The last time I checked, a color on your sign would not accomplish that.

Enterprise Rent-A-Car has been clear about what they are. Obviously, they are a company that rents automobiles – identical cars to the ones the competition provides to customers. Yet when the company broke down the specific points of contact with customers, managers realized that the renter had to obtain possession of the car at some point. At other companies, customers must transport themselves to the rental locations at the airport or a local office. As you know, Enterprise decided their creative step towards distinction was to pick the customer up rather than the typical procedure of the competition. This innovative step – even when the product the customer acquires is precisely the same as what the competition is renting – helped make Enterprise the largest and most successful player in their industry.

Here's another example of driving it down, then picking a point: What ensues when customers pull into your parking lot? Have you even thought about it? Most businesses would say, "Well, good grief, they find a space and park!" Yet businesses dedicated to differentiating themselves will view such a basic action as an opportunity for distinction. They will ask highly detailed questions such as, "Exactly *where* will the customer park?" "How will they know it is the right spot?" And the best approach: "How can we be more creative about showing the customer where to park?"

While working with top BMW car dealers in Europe, I realized how important this seemingly inconsequential point can become. Imagine pulling into the dealership to get your BMW serviced, only to discover a parking lot filled with other BMWs! Where should you park *yours*?

It might seem small to you, but it can be a critical point for your customer. If the customer begins the experience feeling a bit confused, you haven't created the distinction you desire.

Step Three: Develop a Difference

Here is a critical point: to achieve distinction, an organization does not have to become unique in every attribute of what it does. Instead, it has to be creative and develop a difference at a single point that is significant to customers. The differentiation comes from becoming highly creative in at least one single, solitary aspect of its connection with the customer. Such companies have found a point of distinction that creates distance between them and their competitors. And let's face it: by being the first in their business to take this approach, they make it difficult for their competition to duplicate it.

The approach is exactly the same for each of us on an individual level. What strategy can you implement that will create a point of distinction for you with your customers, within the organization, or both?

One manager I know and admire works with her staff to set team goals, and when they are accomplished, the office has a "Film Friday." They'll pop some popcorn and watch a movie on the big screen in the conference room. This manager is beloved by her colleagues. (How many times has business really been like all those football analogies some managers frequently employ? Seldom do we get to act as if we're crossing the goal line and spiking the ball. This manager creates that thrill of achievement for her team.) Imagine being the next manager in that office and attempting to discontinue the practice.

Here's another example: the sales professional who can find a specific point of differentiation in the manner in which he makes a call will find his customers more receptive to his call and his prospects more intrigued by what he has to say.

One representative for a dairy company used to call on Mom and Dad at their grocery store and wear a small flower on his lapel. Every time, without fail, that flower was there. Mom ordered more from him because he was "classy." Dad always noted he was a "real gentleman." As a young and impartial observer, I didn't notice much difference between his milk and cheese from other dairy providers. However, something as simple yet distinctive as a flower in his lapel created a tiny bit of competitive space for him.

How HPU Implements Creativity

Remember HPU's Clarity Statement? "At High Point University, every student receives an extraordinary education in an inspiring environment with caring people." The HPU team then developed creative approaches for each segment of the high concept.

For example, how do you develop an "inspiring environment" and deliver on that promise? Here are five creative steps the University has implemented to follow our Second Cornerstone of Distinction:

1. **Innovative learning spaces:** The university has invested heavily in state-of-the-art facilities like the Plato S. Wilson School of Commerce, Congdon School of Health Sciences, and Nido R. Qubein School of Communication. These spaces are designed to foster engaged, experiential learning.

2. **Engaging campus amenities:** HPU's campus features unique attractions like a movie theater, an arcade, outdoor pools and hot tubs, an ice cream truck, and even a putting green. The goal is to create an immersive, stimulating environment.

3. **Focus on life skills:** In addition to academics, HPU strongly emphasizes teaching life skills through initiatives like the President's Seminar Series, career and professional development services, and a required four-year character development program.

4. **Personalized attention:** HPU touts its low student-faculty ratio and committed faculty who provide mentorship inside and outside the classroom. Concierge staff are available throughout campus to assist students.

5. **Holistic wellness:** The university provides a range of health services and wellness programming to support students' physical, mental, and emotional well-being.

You Can Do the Same

You do not need to change everything about how you do business to create distinction. Often, just ONE creative approach moves you to solve your primary problem.

Start by walking through your list of contact points with customers, reframing and redefining how you perceive each moment of interaction. From these new perspectives, you can create specific points of differentiation with your customers.

By developing your professional laundry list from the exercise—and recognizing that if these practices are the industry standard, they will almost always fail to create distinction for you—you are taking an essential first step in disciplining yourself as a professional to develop differentiated methods and tactics.

The Three Critical Questions for Creativity

1. ***What could you deliver that no competitor is currently doing?***

2. ***What have you changed in the past year or two in what your customers experience when doing business with you? (If you can't think of anything, you're in danger from the third Destroyer of Differentiation: Complacency.)***

3. ***What creative steps could you adapt/adopt from another industry?***

It Shouldn't Be a Secret

However, in addition to the extraordinary benefits it spawns, this second Cornerstone also presents a challenge. Even when you are executing to perfection, all the creativity in the world won't do you or your organization any good if you keep your new, compelling ideas a secret.

It is time to shine! You now have a powerful story to tell. The next chapter will focus on why it is so important to tell it and outline how to do that in today's marketplace to solve your primary problem.

Chapter 5:

The Four Cornerstones of Distinction: Cornerstone #3: Communication

You and your company most likely have access to massive amounts of data on what your customers buy and why. If you own a small business, you are most likely a member of a trade group that can provide you with a comparable amount of research.

The challenge is that only a tiny percentage of these assessments will provide real insight into how you can leverage your clarity—now combined with creativity -- to create unique and specific points of differentiation between you and your competitors—and transform it into communication that genuinely connects with your customers and prospects to solve the primary problem.

We all know of Steve Jobs returning to the company he helped build in a garage, Herb Kelleher designing Southwest Airlines on a cocktail napkin, and Fred Smith getting a C-grade on his master's thesis about the company he wanted to launch that became FedEx.

The difficulty is that while we are captivated by their story, we often neglect our own.

That is a major mistake. It would be a huge error to assume that only a few firms have the history or capacity to tell tales that connect with customers and prospects. Every company and professional has the potential for a captivating narrative.

Communication is the bridge between your business and your audience. It is the vehicle through which you convey your values, mission, and unique value proposition. Effective communication ensures your message reaches and resonates with your audience, creating a solid connection and fostering loyalty. In this chapter, we will explore why telling your story and the elements of a compelling narrative are critical for distinction. We will discuss developing a strong brand voice, highlighting your distinctiveness, and supporting these points with case studies and research.

The Importance of Communication

In today's fast-paced, information-saturated world, clear and compelling communication is more critical than ever. More than having a great product or service is required; you must articulate its value in a way that captures attention and engages your audience. Communication is the key to building brand awareness, trust, and loyalty.

A compelling brand story is one of the most powerful tools in your communication arsenal. It humanizes your brand, makes it relatable, and creates an emotional connection with your audience. Your story should convey who you are, what you stand for, and why your customers should care.

It should be told in a manner that makes your customer the hero – not you or your organization – because your prospects will relate more to the struggles of other customers than they will to your own efforts to stand out.

An exception to this rule is when the company's founding results from
a customer being unable to get what they need or want, so they launch
a business to solve the problem for their situation and others like them.
Many companies have been founded because a single entrepreneur
fervently desired a better product or a better life. Yet, for some mystical
reason, most do not feel that their struggles and challenges merit
conveyance to customers and colleagues. So, they muddle along,
undifferentiated and merely getting by.

In a world where word-of-mouth and social media play significant roles
in shaping brand perceptions, businesses must take control of their
narratives. When you craft compelling, authentic stories that resonate
with your audience, you empower customers to become ambassadors
for your brand, sharing your message consistently and accurately. This
repetition reinforces your brand identity, builds trust, and attracts new
customers through positive endorsements.

On the other hand, if you fail to provide a clear and engaging story,
customers may create their own narratives based on incomplete
information or personal experiences. These self-crafted stories can be
unpredictable and may not align with your brand's values or goals.

By not actively shaping the narrative, you risk losing control over how
your brand is perceived and discussed. It's crucial to intentionally craft
and communicate your stories, ensuring customers have the correct
narrative to share. This ultimately fosters a consistent and positive
brand image for you in the marketplace.

Understanding Story

Joseph Campbell is a significant voice on the power of stories and myth. His work is one of the most important texts available on how to craft compelling, emotionally connecting stories. Campbell's work from the 1940s, *The Hero with a Thousand Faces*, has influenced generations of storytellers, including Star Wars creator George Lucas, who stated that Campbell's approach shaped his blockbuster series of films.

One of Campbell's main points is that for a story to be compelling, the hero cannot begin the narrative as the winner. In other words, a story about your professional or personal efforts—or the growth and development of your organization—cannot begin with your success.

Apple started in the garage, not as a darling of Wall Street; therefore, the return of Steve Jobs as the company was on the brink of extinction makes the story of its success and becoming, perhaps, the world's leading organization an even more gripping narrative.

Campbell said, "A hero is someone who has given his or her life to something bigger than oneself." Only through trials and tribulations— being tested and defeated and then rising to conquer—do we become heroes.

In Homer's *Odyssey*, Ulysses is not a hero at the beginning of the book. It is through facing his trials and challenges that he becomes one. In the New Testament, one way his followers recognized Jesus as divine was through his ability to endure and resist varied forms and incarnations of temptation. The impact of *The Odyssey* or the New Testament would be significantly diminished without the tribulations their heroes successfully overcome.

We are story junkies. We get hooked on good stories. They can be scripted, as soap operas have demonstrated for decades before millions of viewers -- or listeners, in the olden days of radio -- on a daily basis.

The stories can be reality-based, as *The Bachelor*, anything with the Kardashians, and the glut of imitators that have followed have proved. And they can even be grounded in the business world. (Think *Undercover Boss, Shark Tank, The Profit, Undercover Billionaire*, and more.)

Elements of a Compelling Narrative

Before we address how to structure your story, let's first reveal the five elements of a compelling narrative:

1. **Authenticity:** Authenticity is the foundation of a compelling narrative. Your story should be genuine and reflect your true values and mission. Authenticity builds trust and credibility, making your audience more likely to connect with and believe in your brand.

2. **Emotion:** Emotion is a powerful driver of human behavior. A narrative that evokes strong emotions can create a lasting impact and foster a deeper connection with your audience. Whether it's joy, nostalgia, or inspiration, tapping into emotions can make your story more memorable and engaging.

3. **Relatability:** A relatable story resonates with your audience's experiences and aspirations. By understanding your target audience and speaking to their needs and desires, you can craft a narrative that feels personal and relevant.

4. **Conflict and Resolution:** Every great story involves conflict and resolution. Highlighting the challenges your customers have faced and how you've helped them overcome their issues can make your narrative more compelling and showcase your commitment to assisting them.

5. **Vision and Purpose:** A strong narrative communicates your clarity and purpose. It should convey what you stand for and hope to achieve, inspiring your audience to support and join you on your journey.

Example: Airbnb

Airbnb's story is a perfect example of a compelling narrative. It began with the founders renting out air mattresses in their apartment to make some extra money. This simple, relatable beginning evolved into a revolutionary business model that transformed the hospitality industry. Airbnb's story highlights the founders' creativity, resilience, and vision to create a global community of travelers. By sharing this authentic and emotional journey, Airbnb has built a robust and relatable brand that resonates with millions of users worldwide.

The Three-Act Format of Storytelling

If you believe you aren't a storyteller, well, you probably also said in an earlier chapter that you aren't creative, didn't you?

You don't have to be a natural storyteller. You just need to be interested and committed to your story. In today's world, it's not enough to create a story. You must be dedicated to _conveying_ it _repeatedly_ to the groups and individuals who matter most to your organization.

It does you no good whatsoever to craft a story and then fail to spread it through various methods.

You must find the drama and emotion in your story, and the best way to accomplish that goal is through the three-act storytelling format. The three-act format focuses on the two critical elements of every story:

1. _Characters_

2. _The conflict that the characters encounter_

Here is the three-act format:

- Act 1: Introduction of characters and conflict

- Act 2: The varied attempts by the characters to resolve the conflict

- Act 3: The heroic resolution of the conflict by the lead character

Act 1

Introduce your story by revealing characters your audience will find engaging and interesting. Since the beginning of time, storytellers have recognized that the best way to connect us with characters is to place them in a conflict.

The clash can be as dramatic as Montana ranchers trying to preserve their way of life in *Yellowstone* or as wild and twisted as the recent Netflix smash, *Hit Man*. It can take as long to resolve as *War* and Peace or quickly come to a close with a whiter load of laundry that makes for a happy family in a thirty-second Tide commercial. Without the introduction of characters that we care about and a conflict the audience desires to see resolved, what remains of a story has a diminished impact.

Here's how you begin to discover your story:

Start with a blank sheet of paper—we will call this your "story sheet"— and ask yourself, "What conflict did I desire to resolve when I started my business?" Or "What challenge did the company founders seek to conquer when they began?" Or even better, "What problems and conflicts are my customers seeking to resolve?"

For more insight, talk with a favorite client and have them describe the difficulties they encountered before engaging your products and services. Somewhere inside, there is a significant conflict begging for resolution.

Write it down.

Don't rush away from this point. Drill deeply into the conflict before proceeding to the next step.

Remember, if your audience isn't engaged by the characters and conflict in your first act, they won't care what happens in the second.

Act 2

Now that you have defined the conflict, describe the pursuit of an answer to the problem. In the real world, as well as in fiction, few of us arrive at the remedy on our first attempt. Let's face it: any story where the primary character succeeds from the beginning is both a very short and a very dull narrative! You need to describe varied efforts by your characters to resolve the challenges and failures they encountered along the way.

- For example, saying, "Jane was smart and got an A+ in class" is not a compelling story.

- But to vividly describe Jane as growing up in a low-income family that had no high school graduates...and her need for superior grades to gain admission to college as well as her necessity for scholarships to pay for her education...perhaps without the support and understanding of some of her family...as well as her extraordinary efforts to know the material...makes the conclusion "Jane got an A+ in class" a much more captivating narrative.

- **Notice that the results she generated are identical in the two presentations.**

    o   However, adding her efforts, challenges, and situations to the mix—in other words, by creating an act 2—makes the story of Jane's
    A+ infinitely more absorbing.

To use a business model, you could say, "Tom owns a dry-cleaning business."

Or you could point out that Tom, faced with new competition and challenges with environmental regulations, initially became a serious student about, then a leading proponent for, alternative environmentally-friendly cleaning methods. You could describe that he courageously changed the way his parents and grandparents ran the family business. Tom now creatively manages the dry-cleaning establishment in a manner that serves his customers while also becoming a public example of a "green" business.

Note that in both cases, Tom runs a dry-cleaning business. However, by relating a story with an engaging and interesting Act 2, you now present potential customers with a compelling reason to do business with Tom.

To advance your story, you should begin to isolate numerous aspects that detail the search for a resolution that customers, your organization's founders, or you explored or are currently seeking to enhance the impact of your narrative.

Next, write each of these potential facets of your story that you have identified in detail on your "story sheet."

This can be a voluminous quest, as authors James Patterson – not and Ann Napolitano seem to prove with every new book. Or it can be as concise a pursuit as trying to get you to change from your current mobile phone provider to a different one in a half-minute television commercial.

My experience has always been that it is better to start with more examples than you require and then scale your story down so you can streamline your efforts for maximum impact.

Act 3

We have now arrived at the conclusion of your story: the compelling Act

3 and your opportunity to become heroic. However, to maximize the impact of this act, you must take steps to determine how your audience prefers your story to conclude.

I was conducting a consulting session with a team of financial advisors when their experience drove this point home to me. "Scott," the team principal said, "we have always prided ourselves on results and returns that beat the market. And we thought we were doing a pretty good job of telling our clients and prospects that we were doing just that. However, for some reason, we were not getting our messages to have the kind of traction that delivers more of the high-net-worth prospects that any practice desires."

"We would constantly tell them that we were getting higher returns than the market or our competition," he continued, "but it didn't seem to make a difference."

However, when the financial firm changed the conversation to a narrative of a client who faced investment challenges and how their advisors had helped to secure their retirement plans and college funds for their children, their success skyrocketed. It's the power of the story in action.

Consider several wrap-ups to your story. Write them on your "story sheet."

Example: Patagonia

Patagonia excels in using content marketing to tell its brand story. The company's blog, The Cleanest Line, features stories about environmental activism, outdoor adventures, and sustainability initiatives. This content aligns with Patagonia's mission and values, engaging customers who share the same passion for protecting the planet. Patagonia's storytelling through content marketing strengthens its brand identity and fosters a loyal community.

The Next Phase of Distinction for High Point University

Imagine now that High Point University must create a compelling story to communicate its clear and creative points of distinction. How would you do it?

Here is the answer: it would *depend upon the audience.*

A prospective student would prefer a narrative about a young adult facing the pressures of academic performance combined with their desire for an inspiring and enjoyable college experience.

A potential donor might wish to be enthralled by the chronicle of a corporate leader who faces tremendous challenges in finding highly prepared professionals. She then discovers her workforce could become more productive because of the students and graduates of HPU that her company hired.

An article from *Bloomberg BusinessWeek* relates one of the university president's stories to parents:

> *Moving to the edge of the stage, he (Dr. Nido Qubein) picks up a bag of Hershey's Kisses and a box of Godiva chocolates. "The Hershey candy cost about $4," he informs the audience; "the Godiva, $40. Both are good," he says, "but only one resides in the extraordinary. Only one presents itself in a way that people find compelling."*

> *He leans toward the audience, the Godiva box in the palm of his right hand. "Isn't this what you want for your child?"*

Obviously, what one finds moving will leave another cold. This should not come as a surprise. Some movies my wife hates are my favorites, and vice versa. This is why we can go online and discover a variety of movies that are playing to various target audiences. You must customize your story to fit the audience segment you are attempting to attract.

Communication is Essential to Distinction

The adage "Build a better mousetrap, and the world will beat a path to your door" is horribly incorrect and outdated. If the marketplace is unaware of your advantages and cannot Google the path to your doorway, no one will ever arrive to obtain your product. (Besides, fewer customers will "beat a path" to any doorway if they can get it shipped overnight!)

If, however, you have developed *clarity* about who and what you are, *creativity* that generates space between you and your competitors, and if you have *communicated* those results through a compelling story tailored for the precise audiences you desire to attract, you have made significant strides in developing the kind of distinction all organizations and professionals covet.

The Four Critical Questions for Communication

1. ***What is your primary story?***

2. ***How do you tell it?***

3. ***What additional stories can you communicate?***

4. ***What stories are your customers telling their friends and colleagues about you?***

Yet there is one remaining Cornerstone. And it is the one that can propel you and your company to greater heights than perhaps you ever imagined.

Chapter 6:

The Four Cornerstones of Distinction: Cornerstone #4: Customer Experience Focus

Your customers have more choices than ever before. In this environment, the quality of the customer experience often determines whether a business thrives or struggles. An exceptional customer experience goes beyond merely meeting expectations; it involves anticipating customer needs, delivering personalized interactions, and consistently exceeding expectations.

You will never get more customers to spend more money more often and refer you more to friends and colleagues if their experience doing business with you is inferior.

Comedian Jeff Foxworthy was joking about phrases we all utter without thinking. I laughed out loud when he mentioned that people hunting for a lost item often absent-mindedly announce, "I found it in the last place I looked!"

Well, of course you did! Once you come across it, why would you continue searching?

I feel that way when I'm asked whether an organization should focus on customer experience. I always think, "Well, where else could you focus? And why would you keep on searching?" By reiterating the importance of customer experience as a primary focus, you can feel reassured and confident in your business strategy, knowing that you are on the right track.

Think about it for a moment: is it productive to focus internally on the politics and structure of an organization? Obviously, those areas require consideration, examination, and care. But if that's your principal area of concentration, your attention is in the wrong place. It won't answer the question posed at the beginning of this book: ***"Does this compel more customers to spend more money more often and provide us with more referrals?"***

The same is true if your organization's focal point is on the market and your share price. From a historical perspective, we know that organizations that are distinctive from their competition are the winners in the marketplace over the long haul. However, when viewed through the lens of daily trading, the market often tends to reward incremental, short-term gains. If you're always centered on what your shares are doing right now, you are likely missing long-term opportunities that will solve your primary problem.

Aren't Service and Experience the Same?

Many organizations have yet to explore the fundamental difference between providing customer service and creating a customer experience. This often occurs because there are three independent and distinct levels of customer interaction. For an organization to excel, it must examine these levels separately and create a plan to strategically improve performance at each level.

- ***Level One: Processing:*** the *essential* elements of the transaction; the aspects your customer has a right to expect you to deliver because they have chosen to spend money with you and your organization.

- **_Level Two:_** Service: the steps you and your organization will undertake to make processing frictionless, more efficient, palatable, enjoyable, and/or friendly to enhance the likelihood that customers will repeat their business.

- **_Level Three:_** Experience: the commitment to and execution of specific personalization strategies required to create the element of emotion. This results in an intense connection with customers. _Loyalty from the client toward your organization is only generated at Level Three._ (What incentive do I have to develop loyalty towards something to which I feel no emotional connection?)

Progressive Attainment of Customer Interaction Success

The attainment of these levels of customer interaction is progressive. If you fail in processing—for example, if the food at your restaurant isn't properly prepared or if I had to wait an extended period after the time I had reserved my table—then the higher levels of interaction have little traction.

If my flight arrives at O'Hare three hours late, I really don't care how hot the coffee tastes on the flight. However, when the flight is on time and uneventful, receiving a nice cup of java enhances my evaluation of your airline's ability to provide me with what I want.

This morning, I went into a local coffee store called Old Crown to pick up my wife Tammy's favorite morning beverage. I think it's a pretty complicated concoction. She wants an iced mocha with oat milk, an extra shot of espresso, and just a light touch of fat-free whipped cream on top.

This morning's drink was prepared perfectly (level one: _processing_). The line in the Old Crown moved quickly, and the place is a clean and inviting environment (level two: _service_). When I approached the counter,

I was greeted with, "Good morning, Mr. McKain! How's the book coming along?" (You can imagine that when you are working hard to complete a manuscript, it's an emotional moment to have someone concerned!)

And at the point where the barista behind the machine asked, "Picking up the usual drink for Tammy?" I had absolutely reached the point of experience. All I had to do was ask for Tammy's "usual," and the barista knew the formula for her favorite drink.

That's not just a customer-service focus—it's a customer-experience focus.

As I'm writing this, I realize I don't know if the iced mochas are more or less expensive at Old Crown than at Starbucks or other coffee shops serving a similar drink. *However, this is the critical point for me: my experience at Old Crown makes it irrelevant.*

For the owners of Old Crown, here's the vital aspect: I'm now a customer who comes back more often, spends more, and refers them more frequently to friends and colleagues. Hey, I'm telling <u>you</u> right now!

The Courage Required for Customer Commitment

I'm currently working with an organization that has had a leadership transition. The new CEO is completely committed to changing the organization's culture and putting a stake in the ground that his leadership legacy will be one of a concerted and disciplined focus on the client experience.

The challenge is that many of his managers believe this is a "nice" approach, but they want to delegate the effort of customer experiences to a single client-services department.

One manager even told me he wanted the "client-facing people to take care of the customers so I can just do my job." I'm convinced that if this manager truly believes customers in today's marketplace are somebody else's job, then he should be out of a job!

If you are unsuccessful in solving your primary problem in the marketplace through the Four Cornerstones—particularly this one—then it practically becomes ensured that a mediocre voyage on the sea of sameness is the best you'll be able to achieve. Please understand, too, that abject failure is a definite possibility.

I admire the new CEO, but my esteem is slight compared to how his colleagues will respect and appreciate him in a short time. He not only has an opportunity to lead an organization, he is taking advantage of a chance to pioneer a new level of client connectivity and distinction in his industry.

If you are the leader of a company—regardless of its size—do you have similar courage and commitment?

The Ultimate Customer Experience®

What if you and your organization took this Cornerstone to the limit? What if you decided to deliver the ultimate experience?

The Ultimate Customer Experience® is not just the title of a previous book of mine or a federally registered trademark of our company. It's not merely buzzwords. It is a critical element for achieving distinction in today's crowded marketplace. Focusing on delivering it will set you apart from the competition, foster loyalty, and drive long-term business success.

Envisioning the Ultimate Customer Experience® (UCX) involves at least four key components:

1. *Understanding your customers*

2. *Personalizing interactions*

3. *Ensuring consistency across all touchpoints*

4. *Continuously seeking feedback to improve*

Understanding Your Customers

The foundation of a UCX is a deep understanding of your customers. This involves knowing their preferences, pain points, and expectations. Use data and analytics to gain insights into customer behavior and tailor your interactions accordingly.

Example: Stitch Fix

Stitch Fix, an online personal styling service, uses data and algorithms to understand customers' preferences and style choices. By analyzing customer feedback and purchase history, Stitch Fix provides personalized clothing recommendations that cater to individual tastes. This data-driven approach has helped Stitch Fix build a loyal customer base and deliver a highly personalized shopping experience.

Personalizing Interactions

Personalization is critical to making customers feel valued and understood. Use customer data to tailor your communications, offers, and services to individual needs. Personalization can range from email addressing customers by their names to offering product recommendations based on past purchases.

Example: Sephora

Sephora excels at personalization through its Beauty Insider program. The program tracks customers' preferences, purchase history, and beauty profiles to provide tailored product recommendations and exclusive offers. Sephora's personalized emails, app notifications, and in-store experiences create a cohesive and engaging customer journey, fostering loyalty and repeat business.

Ensuring Consistency Across Touchpoints

Consistency is crucial for building trust and delivering a UCX. Ensure that your brand message, values, and quality of service are consistent across all customer touchpoints, including your website, social media, customer service, and physical locations.

Example: Trader Joe's

Trader Joe's is known for its consistent customer experience across all its stores. From friendly and knowledgeable staff to unique product offerings and a quirky, fun atmosphere, every Trader Joe's location delivers the same high-quality experience. This consistency has helped Trader Joe's build a strong, loyal customer base and a distinct brand identity.

Continuously Seeking Feedback

Customer feedback is invaluable for understanding what works and what needs improvement in your customer experience strategy. Regularly seek feedback through surveys, reviews, and direct interactions, and use this information to make data-driven improvements.

Example: Zappos

Zappos is renowned for its commitment to exceptional customer experiences. The company actively seeks customer feedback through surveys, social media, and direct interactions with its customer service team. Zappos uses this feedback to continually refine its processes and ensure that every customer interaction meets the highest standards of service. This relentless focus has made Zappos a benchmark for customer experience excellence.

Five Specific Steps to the Ultimate Customer Experience®

Here's a brief, five-step look at how you can implement the UCX for your organization:

Step One: Ask the Question

The first step to creating the UCX is to take a legal pad and ask, individually or with your team, this question: "What would have to happen for everything to go *exactly* right?"

Then, record all responses.

Doing this is more complex than it might first appear. For example, if everything went "exactly right," you would also need to ask questions like:

- *How many times would the phone ring before it was answered?*

- *What percentage of your calls should be fielded by a live person instead of via technology?*

- *What sensations would be experienced by customers when they walk into your store?*

  o   *What would the temperature be?*

  o   *What would customers hear?*

    ☐   *In other words, what should the store sound and feel like?*

The most critical factor here is to keep drilling down to the smallest aspects of your interactions with customers and prospects. Constantly push for what would have to happen for that contact to be *exactly* right.

Legend states that Starbucks prohibits its associates from wearing cologne or perfume on their workdays. The reason is apparent. When you walk into the coffee shop, Starbucks wants you to savor the aroma of the coffee, not wonder if you are inhaling Dior's J'Adore or Versace Dylan Blue.

You must examine every aspect of your interactions with customers and prospects with extraordinary precision to get it exactly right. That's the standard of the Ultimate Customer Experience.

Step Two: Engage Your Customer in the Process

It is essential that you involve your customers in the process of creating the UCX. After all, how can it be "ultimate" if it fails to deliver what the customer really wants?

When interaction is enhanced, connectivity follows.

The most basic—and most powerful—approach to involving the customer is to ask them: **"If you could describe the ultimate experience of doing business with an organization like ours, what would that be?"** Then you *listen!*

Many face the underlying problem with this approach to customers: Simply listening to them at this point appears counterproductive. When a customer responds, you have the opportunity to initiate a transaction. As a result, you may find it difficult to refuse the opportunity to "close the sale."

For example, as your client responds to your UCX query, she may declare that she wants something that you already offer. Your natural tendency could be to butt in and declare, "We do that!" At this point, from the customer's perspective, the entire process appears to be nothing more than a smart sales pitch—not an effort to improve their customer experience.

Furthermore, you are unwittingly hindering the relationship. Customers, like friends and relatives, want to be heard and appreciated. When you try to push the consumer and complete a purchase, you may miss out on hearing extraordinarily insightful and revealing information that could lead to them spending more with you more often.

Step Three: Sync the Information

Next, compare the processes you defined internally to produce the UCX to the goals and dreams shared by your customers.

In some instances, the two may complement each other—that is, what the customers told you they wanted in the UCX and what you detailed throughout your process may be very compatible.

However, certain outcomes can be quite contradictory. If this is the case, remember you're designing the UCX to engage your customers! You must grant them the benefit of the doubt. On the other hand, you must temper this with the understanding that your vision of the future may be more advanced and profound than currently available to your customers. Your insight is indispensable to constructing the UCX.

Step Four: Outline the Roadblocks

Another vital question to the development of the UCX is: "What roadblocks prevent us from executing the Ultimate Customer Experience for every customer or prospect at every point of interaction?" Make a list of as many barriers as you can. Then, investigate and analyze each of them.

Some will be outdated corporate policies, while others will be misguided strategies. All these UCX obstructions should be intensely scrutinized and, hopefully, eliminated.

Step Five: Execute!

If only it were that simple, right?

Look, I know that none of us—no matter our position within the company, from owner to custodian—can snap our fingers and implement a strategy. The Ultimate Customer Experience almost always boils down to a commitment made by employees throughout an organization.

It's the Performance at Each Touchpoint

A few days ago, an airline employee stood behind the ticket kiosk with my driver's license in one hand and a computer screen with my reservation in front of her. She was literally surrounded by information with my name on it, yet she never used "Scott" or "McKain" at any point in our interaction.

It's impossible to create an experience—much less the UCX—without those with direct engagement with the customer properly executing at these little points of contact. The CEO can insist upon it, yet if a frontline employee does not actually deliver it, the customer will fail to feel as if their experience is customer-focused.

However, please consider this: why do you suppose we constantly read and hear about the same companies? You know the ones: Starbucks, Apple, Amazon, Southwest, and Nordstrom. The reason is simply because so unbelievably few organizations execute on the promise of the Ultimate Customer Experience. That's how breathtakingly difficult it is.

However, the spectacular success of a few organizations should also clearly display how critical it is for all of us to endeavor to deliver the

UCX. Customers who experience a UCX with a brand are more likely to return and make repeat purchases. Customers who receive personalized and consistent experiences are more likely to spend more over their lifetime with you. They are also more likely to explore additional products or services your company offers. Happy customers will likely share their positive experiences with friends and family, generating valuable word-of-mouth marketing. In contrast, dissatisfied customers can harm your reputation through negative reviews and feedback posted online on a variety of methods, from social media platforms to Google and Yelp.

Research and Statistics

A Nielsen report found that 92% of consumers trust recommendations from friends and family over any other type of advertising. This highlights the power of positive word-of-mouth in influencing purchasing decisions.

According to a study by PwC, 73% of consumers cite customer experience as an essential factor in their purchasing decisions, yet only 49% of U.S. consumers say companies provide a good customer experience.

Furthermore, a Salesforce report found that 80% of customers consider a company's experience as important as its products and services. These statistics underscore the critical role of customer experience in influencing consumer behavior and driving business success.

It's the Way You Do Business

High Point University would never be the same if President Qubein announced at a faculty and staff meeting, "Admissions and endowment goals have been exceeded, so don't worry about that 'inspiring environment' stuff anymore. Just do your jobs." In fact, Dr. Qubein would be the first to dramatically emphasize to his team that creating the inspiring environment is their job—it is their version of the UCX, and it's just how things are done at HPU.

Ritz-Carlton is synonymous with luxury and exceptional customer service and is an often-used example. The hotel's commitment to personalized service and attention to detail has set it apart in the hospitality industry. Ritz-Carlton's "Ladies and Gentlemen" philosophy empowers employees to anticipate and fulfill guests' needs, creating memorable experiences that drive repeat business and brand loyalty. It's just the way things are done at Ritz-Carlton.

REI fosters a Customer Experience Focus by aligning its mission and values with the customer experience. The company's commitment to quality products, environmental stewardship, and community engagement resonates with its customers. REI employees, known as "Green Vests," are passionate about outdoor activities and provide knowledgeable, personalized service that enhances the customer experience. It's just how things are done at REI.

What About You?

If I asked your customers about "the way things are done" at your business, would they express in their own words that you are distinctive and deliver an Ultimate Customer Experience?

- Would they be able, in their terms, to describe what makes you stand out from the competition?

- Will they tell me that they plan to make more frequent purchases and tell more friends and colleagues about you?

- Or would they say they can't tell much difference between you and your competition?

- Would their description indicate you are solving your primary problem or remaining adrift in a sea of sameness?

- **How would they describe the way you do business?**

The Five Critical Questions for Customer Experience Focus

1. *What do you want your customers to feel when they do business with you?*

2. *What if everything went exactly right?*

3. *What must you do to make it work that way and deliver an Ultimate Customer Experience?*

4. *What roadblocks prevent the execution of a UCX for every customer every time?*

5. *How are you training and educating your team to ensure this experience is delivered on the front lines of your business?*

Chapter 7:

Solving Your Primary Problem

Each cornerstone we've explored—Clarity, Creativity, Communication, and Customer Experience Focus—plays a vital role in creating distinction and driving extraordinary growth for your business. By embracing these principles, you can transform your organization, attract more customers, and achieve lasting success.

Let's briefly revisit each cornerstone and its importance before we conclude with a call to action to conquer your primary problem and chart a fresh course to success.

Clarity: Understanding Your Identity

Clarity is the foundation upon which all other elements of distinction are built. It involves precisely understanding who you are, who you aren't, what you do, and what makes you unique. Without clarity, your marketing messages can become muddled, and your value proposition can be lost on potential customers.

Research and Statistics

Companies with clear and well-communicated values see a 27% increase in performance and a 50% increase in employee engagement. This underscores the significant impact that clarity can have on your business success.

Creativity: Fueling Innovation

Creativity is the spark that ignites innovation and sets your business apart from the competition. We explored how creativity drives the development of new products, services, and business models that capture the imagination of your customers.

Key Components of Creativity

We discussed several critical components of fostering creativity within your organization:

1. **Encouraging Experimentation:** Creating a culture that values experimentation and embraces failure as a learning opportunity.

2. **Encouraging Diverse Perspectives:** Leveraging diverse backgrounds and experiences to generate innovative ideas.

3. **Creating an Environment that Stimulates Creativity:** Designing workspaces that inspire and facilitate collaboration.

4. **Investing in Creative Development:** Providing opportunities for continuous learning and creative expression.

Research and Statistics

Research shows that companies prioritizing breakthrough innovation over incremental improvements are more likely to achieve market leadership. A report by Boston Consulting Group found that such companies are 2.5 times more likely to be top performers in their industry.

Communication: Telling Your Story

Effective communication is essential for building a solid connection with your audience and conveying your unique value proposition. Chapter 5 discussed the importance of telling your story and the elements of a compelling narrative.

We identified several key elements of a compelling brand narrative:

5. **Authenticity:** Being genuine and reflecting your true values and mission.

6. **Emotion:** Evoking strong emotions to create a lasting impact.

7. Relatability: Crafting a story that resonates with your audience's experiences and aspirations.

8. **Conflict and Resolution:** Highlighting challenges and how you've overcome them.

9. **Vision and Purpose:** Communicating your vision and purpose to inspire your audience.

We also revealed the Three-Act approach to creating a compelling story:

- Act 1: Introduction of characters and conflict

- Act 2: The varied attempts by the characters to resolve the conflict

- Act 3: The heroic resolution of the conflict by the lead character

A study by Sprout Social found that 76% of consumers expect brands to be consistent across all touchpoints, highlighting the importance of a cohesive communication strategy. Consistent and compelling communication can significantly enhance your brand's visibility and customer engagement.

Customer Experience Focus: Delivering the Ultimate Customer Experience®

The Ultimate Customer Experience® is critical for distinction. It involves consistently exceeding customer expectations, personalizing interactions, and creating memorable experiences. Chapter 6 explored how focusing on customer experience can set your business apart and drive long-term success.

Key Strategies for the Ultimate Customer Experience®

We identified several strategies for delivering an exceptional customer experience:

1. **Understanding Your Customers:** Gaining insights into customer preferences, pain points, and expectations.

2. **Personalizing Interactions:** Tailoring communications, offers, and services to individual needs.

3. **Ensuring Consistency Across Touchpoints:** Maintaining a consistent brand message and quality of service across all channels.

4. **Continuously Seeking Feedback:** Regularly gather and act on customer feedback to improve the experience.

Research and Statistics

According to a study by Bain & Company, increasing customer retention rates by 5% increases profits by 25% to 95%. This demonstrates the significant financial impact of building customer loyalty through exceptional experiences. Additionally, a report by Salesforce found that 80% of customers consider the experience a company provides as important as its products and services.

Bringing It All Together: The Path to Distinction

The journey to distinction involves integrating these four cornerstones—Clarity, Creativity, Communication, and Customer Experience Focus—into every aspect of your business. Doing so creates a cohesive and compelling brand that resonates with your audience and stands out in the marketplace.

A study by Adobe found that companies fostering creativity achieve 1.5 times higher market share and 3.5 times higher revenue growth than their peers. Additionally, organizations that effectively measure and analyze their communication efforts are 2.6 times more likely to achieve their business goals. These findings highlight the powerful impact of integrating clarity, creativity, communication, and customer experience focus to drive business success.

Taking the Next Step

Now that we've explored the four cornerstones of distinction, it's time to take action. Implementing these strategies requires commitment, effort, and a willingness to embrace change. Here are some steps to get started:

- **Assess Your Current Position**

    o   Conduct a thorough assessment of your current business practices. Identify areas where you excel and areas that need improvement.

    o   Use tools like SWOT analysis to evaluate your strengths, weaknesses, opportunities, and threats.

- **Define Your Clarity Statement**

    o   If you haven't already, take the time to define or refine your Clarity Statement.

    o   Ensure it reflects your core values and long-term goals.

    o   Communicate these statements to your team and ensure everyone is aligned with your vision.

- **Foster a Culture of Creativity**

  o   Encourage creativity and innovation within your organization.

  o   Create an environment that supports experimentation, values diverse perspectives, and invests in continuous learning and development.

- **Craft Your Story**

  o   Develop a compelling narrative that tells your story.

  o   Ensure it is authentic, emotional, relatable, and purpose-driven.

  o   Use this story as the foundation for your marketing and communication efforts.

- **Focus on the Customer Experience**

  o   Prioritize the customer experience at every touchpoint.

  o   Understand your customers, personalize interactions, maintain consistency, and continuously seek feedback to improve.

  o   Empower your employees to deliver exceptional service and create memorable experiences.

- **Measure and Refine**

  o   Measure the impact of your efforts regularly using both qualitative and quantitative metrics.

  o   Use this data to refine your strategies and ensure continuous improvement.

The Journey Ahead

Remember, the journey to solve your primary problem and create distinction is ongoing. It requires dedication, creativity, and a relentless focus on your customers. But the rewards are well worth the effort.

By embracing the four cornerstones of *Clarity, Creativity, Communication,* and *Customer Experience Focus,* you can create a business that stands out, attracts more customers, and achieves extraordinary growth.

I encourage you to apply the insights and strategies we've discussed to your business. Be bold, be innovative, and always keep your customers at the heart of everything you do. The path to distinction is within your reach. Embrace it and watch your business soar to new heights.

Thank you for joining me on this journey. I look forward to seeing the remarkable impact you will make as you create distinction and deliver the Ultimate Customer Experience®. Your business deserves to be valued for what makes it unique. Let's make it happen.

Final Thoughts

1. **Take Action:** Implement the strategies discussed to enhance clarity, foster creativity, improve communication, and elevate the customer experience.

2. **Stay Committed:** Continuously evaluate and refine your approach to ensure ongoing improvement and success.

3. **Inspire Your Team:** Share your vision and goals with your team and inspire them to join you in creating distinction and delivering exceptional customer experiences.

The easiest approach is to merely continue what you are currently doing. You may perceive that "don't make waves" and "keep on keeping on" are the safest things for you to do. Let me emphatically state my belief that this is the most dangerous approach in the vast majority of cases!

Because of the Three Destroyers of Differentiation, your job will only continue to become more difficult, both from an organizational and an individual perspective.

However, if you start today to chart a fresh approach based on the Four Cornerstones of Distinction, you can enhance your organization while nurturing and growing yourself.

The future of your business lies in your hands. You can achieve distinction and drive extraordinary growth with dedication, innovation, and a customer-centric mindset. Embark on this exciting journey together and create a legacy of excellence.

You'll discover that your customers start spending more money more often and referring your business more to their friends and colleagues.

Conquer your primary problem!

OTHER BOOKS BY SCOTT McKAIN

- The Ultimate Customer Experience:5 Steps Everyone Must Know to Excite Your Customers, Engage Your Colleagues, and Enjoy Your Work

- ICONIC: How Organizations and Leaders Attain, Sustain, and Regain the Ultimate Level of Distinction

- All Business Is Still Show Business: Create Distinction and Earn Standing Ovations from Customers in a Hyper-Competitive Marketplace

- Create Distinction: What to Do When "Great" Isn't Good Enough to Grow Your Business

- 7 Tenets of Taxi Terry: How Every Employee Can Create and Deliver the Ultimate Customer Experience

- Collapse of Distinction: Stand Out and Move Up While Your Competition Fails

- What Customers Really Want: How to Bridge the Gap Between What Your Organization Offers and What Your Clients Crave

- All Business Is Show Business: Strategies For Earning Standing Ovations from Your Customers

- Just Say Yes: A Step Up to Success! (with Antonia Barnes Boyle)

HAVE SCOTT McKAIN SPEAK AT YOUR NEXT EVENT!

Here's why you should have Scott McKain keynote your next event or virtual conference:

You will get more than a speech: Attendees (both for in-person or online events) begin learning before Scott's presentation with our interactive pre-event program. Our post-event offerings ensure Scott's message has an impact long after your meeting concludes.

You will receive custom content: There are no canned presentations. Every talk is custom-designed and relevant to each audience.

You will benefit from his wealth of experience: Scott's vast experience in many industries means he can cherry-pick optimal solutions from a wide array of distinctive organizations and professionals in a way that an expert in a single sector simply cannot.

You'll love his unique style: Almost 70 percent of his bookings are from repeat clients—astonishing for a keynoter and the reason why Scott is one of the world's most in-demand speakers. Clients ask him to return, and they tell their friends about him! Scott is the highest-rated speaker in the history of many distinctive organizations.

We offer multiple ways to serve you! Scott offers everything from in-depth, ongoing educational programs delivered online and in-person to keynote speeches and content-rich seminars. He is also a highly successful consultant and professional coach. Scott's company has myriad formats ready to customize specifically for your organization's unique needs.

We would love to assist you in solving your primary problem and help your organization to create distinction!

ABOUT SCOTT McKAIN

Scott McKain is an internationally known distinction expert, bestselling author, and iconic keynote speaker. Scott's unique platform style has earned him induction into the Professional Speakers Hall of Fame, and his remarkable content earned him membership (along with Dale Carnegie, Zig Ziglar, and Og Mandino) as one of only twenty-four people selected for inclusion in the Sales and Marketing Hall of Fame.

He is currently "In Residence Expert on Distinction and Relevance" at High Point University, named by U.S. News & World Report as the nation's "most innovative" university.

Scott has over three decades of research and experience. He has spoken and consulted for the world's most influential corporations, presenting his business strategies on platforms in all fifty states and forty countries.

Scott McKain's book ICONIC was named a Forbes "Top 10 Pick of the Year." It is an instruction guide for professionals and organizations to become so distinctive that they not only stand out in their industry but also set the benchmark for innovation, customer experience, and employee culture.

Scott and his wife, Tammy, reside in Las Vegas, Nevada, and Fort Wayne, Indiana.

Have Scott McKain Speak At Your Next Event!

For more information, visit
ScottMcKain.com

9 798218 463403